History Alive!
Interactive Student
Notebook

Teachers' Curriculum Institute
Creators of *History Alive!*
P.O. Box 50996
Palo Alto, CA 94303
(800) 497-6138
www.historyalive.com

ISBN 1-58371-002-7

6 7 8 9 10 03 02

Contents

Contents

Interactive Student Notebooks

During this one-day workshop, teachers will learn how to

- apply the three premises of the History Alive! program—cooperative interaction, multiple intelligences, and the spiral curriculum—to reach all students

- inspire students to become academically organized by giving them clear guidelines for creating high-quality notebooks

- help students use the right side of a spiral notebook to record notes from lectures, discussions, and readings and the left side to process that information in creative and engaging ways

- properly introduce and sequence notebook assignments to help students see how class activities connect to one another

- create engaging notebook assignments

- assess completed student notebooks

- encourage students to take pride in their notebooks so they will refer to them often and seldom lose them

The Three Premises of History Alive!

"To my mind, a human intellectual competence must entail a set of skills of problem solving and also entail the potential for finding or creating problems."

Howard Gardner
Frames of Mind: The Theory of Multiple Intelligences

"To my mind, a human intellectual competence must entail a set of skills of problem solving and also entail the potential for finding or creating problems."

Howard Gardner
Frames of Mind: The Theory of Multiple Intelligences

1 Students have different learning styles. Howard Gardner's findings that human cognition includes a far wider and more universal set of competencies than had previously been recognized offer the possibility of revolutionizing the instruction of history in our schools. Gardner has found that every student excels in several of the seven intelligences.

If we accept this premise, we will begin to discover that the cognitive capabilities of our students are much richer and more varied than we had previously imagined. Recognizing this plurality of intelligences means rethinking the assumption that students are generally either "smart" or "slow." According to the theory of multiple intelligences, every student is intelligent—just not in the same way. Gardner's research has identified these seven intelligences:

- Verbal-Linguistic
- Logical-Mathematical
- Visual-Spatial
- Body-Kinesthetic
- Musical-Rhythmic
- Interpersonal
- Intrapersonal

2 **Cooperative interaction increases learning and improves social skills.**   The second theoretical premise behind the History Alive! approach can be easily stated: cooperative interaction leads to learning gains. Researchers report that cooperative groupwork promotes higher student achievement and that increased student interaction leads to more learning and retention.

However, sociologists have found that when students perform a groupwork task, they prejudge what their peers will be able to contribute on the basis of perceived academic ability and peer status. Perceived "high status" students tend to interpret most of the questions, to talk more, and to have their opinions accepted more than perceived "low status" students. The high-status students, because they interact more, learn more; the low-status students, because their interaction is severely limited, learn less. It is a classic example of the rich getting richer and the poor getting poorer.

Elizabeth Cohen's research has uncovered practical ways to combat this problem. She has found that if students are trained in cooperative norms and behaviors, placed in heterogeneous small groups, and assigned specific roles to complete during a multiple-ability task, they tend to interact more equally.

3 **All students can learn.**   The third theoretical premise behind the History Alive! approach is the idea of the spiral curriculum. Championed by educational theorist Jerome Bruner, the spiral curriculum is based on the belief that all students can learn if a teacher shows them how to think and to discover knowledge for themselves. Students learn progressively more difficult concepts through a process of step-by-step self-discovery.

"Groupwork is an effective technique for achieving certain kinds of intellectual and social learning goals. It is a superior technique for conceptual learning, for creative problem solving, and for increasing oral language proficiency."

Elizabeth Cohen
Designing Groupwork Strategies for the Heterogeneous Classroom

"Any subject can be taught effectively in some intellectually honest form to any child at any stage of development. Through a spiral curriculum students learn progressively more difficult concepts through step-by-step self-discovery."

Jerome Bruner
The Process of Education

Introduction

Interactive Student Notebooks

Many student notebooks are drab repositories of information filled with uninspired, unconnected, and poorly understood ideas. Interactive Student Notebooks, however, allow students to record information about history in an engaging way. As students learn new ideas, they use several types of writing and innovative graphic techniques to record them. They then process those ideas—for example, they might transform written concepts into visuals, find the main point of a political cartoon, or organize historical events into a topical net. This encourages students to use their critical-thinking skills to organize information and ponder historical questions. As a result, students become more creative, more independent thinkers.

The first time you see an Interactive Student Notebook, you will notice colorful and varied expression. Words and diagrams, bullets and arrows, ink and pencil, a multitude of colors, and highlighting are all presented in a unique, personal style.

Traditional student notebooks may work for motivated students with strong linguistic skills, but they do not serve students who have other learning styles. In Interactive Student Notebooks, key ideas are underlined in color or highlighted; Venn diagrams show relationships; cartoon sketches show people and events; timelines illustrate chronology; indentations and bullets indicate subordination; arrows show cause-and-effect relationships. Students develop graphical thinking skills, and those who were alienated in the conventional classroom are often motivated to understand and express high-level concepts.

Materials

To create Interactive Student Notebooks, students must bring these materials to class each day:

- their 8 ½-by-11-inch spiral-bound notebook, with at least 100 pages
- a pen
- a pencil with an eraser
- two felt-tip pens of different colors
- two highlighters of different colors
- a container for all of these (purse, backpack, vinyl packet)

Tell students that these additional materials would be helpful:

- a variety of colored pens
- several more highlighters
- a small pair of scissors
- rubber cement or a glue stick

Give students three or four days to purchase these materials. By buying their own materials, students will take ownership of their notebooks and will be less likely to lose them. Even students with limited financial resources should be encouraged to purchase their own materials.

Right-side, Left-side Orientation

Interactive Student Notebooks encourage students to record notes in an organized, logical fashion and to work with and process the information in ways that help them better understand history.

The right side of the notebook—the "input" side—is used for recording class notes, discussion notes, and reading notes. Typically, all "testable" information is found here. Historical information can be organized in the form of traditional outline notes. However, the right side of the notebook is also an excellent place for the teacher to model how to think graphically by using illustrated outlines, flow charts, annotated slides, T-charts, and other graphic organizers.

The right side of the notebook

- provides an opportunity for the teacher to model for students how to think graphically. There are many visual ways to organize historical information that enhance understanding.
- is where the teacher organizes a common set of information that all students must know.

Your Students' Notebooks Will Improve over Time

Teaching students how to use Interactive Student Notebooks is a complex task. It takes patience, good modeling, and constant reinforcement. You will discover that after two or three semesters, your students' notebooks will improve dramatically. This teaching skill takes time to learn, so give yourself that luxury.

The left side—the "output" side—is primarily used for processing new ideas. Students work out an understanding of new material by using illustrations, diagrams, flow charts, poetry, colors, matrices, cartoons, and the like. Students explore their opinions and clarify their values on controversial issues, wonder about "what if" hypothetical situations, and ask questions about new ideas. They also express their feelings and reactions to activities that tap into intrapersonal learning. And they review what they have learned and preview what they will learn. By doing so, students are encouraged to see how individual lessons fit into the larger context of a unit.

The left side of the notebook

- stresses that writing down lecture notes does not mean students have learned the information. They must actively *do* something with the information before they internalize it.
- clearly indicates which ideas are the teacher's and which are the student's. Everything on the left side is the student's.
- gives students permission to be playful and experimental since they know the left side is their page and they will not be interfering with class notes.
- allows students to use various learning styles to process information.

Left Side
Student Processing
"Output"

Right Side
Teacher Directed
"Input"

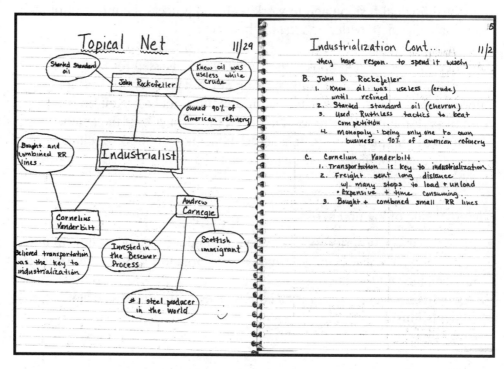

Here is a simple example of the right-side, left-side orientation of the Interactive Student Notebook in action. The student began by taking class notes on late nineteenth-century industrialism on the right side of her notebook and then, for homework, completed a topical net on the corresponding left side using information from class notes.

Why Interactive Student Notebooks Engage Students

Students use both their visual and linguistic intelligences. In these notebooks, students approach understanding in many ways. As they grapple with new ideas, they will use several types of writing and several graphic techniques. The left side allows visual learners to use their best medium to explore and to share ideas, and encourages nonvisual learners to become more proficient with graphic approaches in a nonthreatening way. Likewise, both types of learners will work with their writing skills. All students benefit from this two-pronged approach.

Note taking becomes an active process. These notebooks reach out to students, inviting them to become engaged in their learning. Students will devote some time to passively recording ideas from a lecture or the board, but most of the time they are *doing* something with ideas: putting them into their own words, searching for implications or assumptions, transforming words into visuals, finding the main point of a political cartoon. This is especially true on the left side of the notebook, which is reserved for the students' active exploration of ideas.

Notebooks help students to systematically organize as they learn. Encourage students to use their notebooks to record ideas about every activity they engage in during a unit. Have them use organizational techniques—topic headings, colored highlights, different writing styles— to synthesize historical concepts.

Notebooks become a portfolio of individual learning. These personal, creative notebooks become a record of each student's growth. The teacher, students, and even families can review a student's progress in writing, graphic, recording, and organization skills.

Help Students to See the Coherent Whole

Because the Interactive Student Notebook allows students to group assignments by unit, students begin to see a logical flow from assignment to assignment and to understand the coherence of a unit. Their notebooks serve as a chronological record of their work and help reinforce the major concepts and themes in a unit.

Notebooks allow students to express their ideas, questions, and feelings in a host of creative ways. No two effective Interactive Student Notebooks look the same. Nonetheless, an effective notebook usually has some basic elements—a cover, a set of clear guidelines for students, a contents page, and title pages for each new unit—that give students the structure they need to allow their individual styles to flourish.

Covers

Introduce the Interactive Student Notebook by encouraging students to create colorful and fun covers that reflect the course content. This immediately sends them the message that the notebooks will be their own creations that they can take pride in, which will help cut down on the number of lost notebooks throughout the school year.

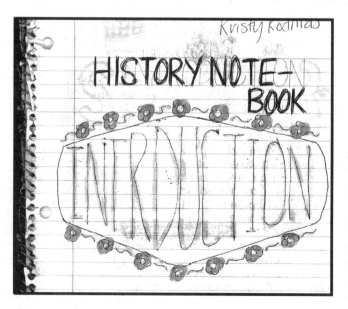

This notebook cover is missing key information such as the actual name of the course, the class period, and the date. Missing information makes your job harder when it comes time to grade notebooks. It is critical that you set clear criteria for every assignment and element of the Interactive Student Notebook.

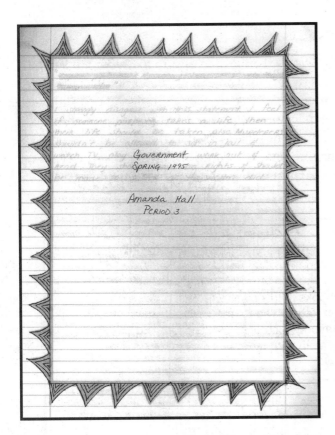

An effective cover can have a simple, elegant design as long as it includes the basics: course name, date, class period, and student's name.

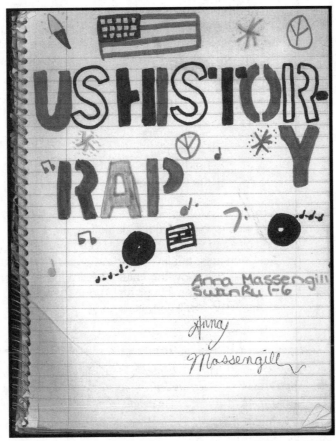

Although not apparent in this black-and-white reproduction, this student used bold colors to draw attention to her basic history design elements.

The Right First Steps

Before students complete their first assignment in their notebooks, have them save ten pages in the front for creating a cumulative table of contents. You may also want to have them number all the pages in their notebooks immediately so they can be organized right from the start.

Student Guidelines

One of the most important steps you can take to ensure that your students create successful notebooks is to set clear notebook guidelines. Decide ahead of time what you expect your students to produce in their notebooks and then clearly communicate these expectations to them. Most teachers create a list of criteria and ask students to tape or glue that list to the inside covers of their spiral notebooks. Some teachers include directions for specific types of notebook assignments, class rules, and even the class grading policy.

Showcase Great Notebooks

Showcase exceptional notebooks so students have the opportunity to gather ideas for improving their own notebooks. You might set up six or eight stations around the classroom and put an outstanding notebook at each station. Allow students 15 or 20 minutes to roam around the room and collect ideas from these model notebooks.

Guidelines for Interactive Student Notebooks
World Studies, Period 1

Introduction: Notebooks in this class will have a "left side, right side" orientation to help you record, organize, and process new information. Much of your classwork and homework will be done in your notebook. Notebooks will be organized in this way:

Left Side Students Process New Ideas	Right Side Teacher Provides New Info
• Reorganize new info in creative formats • Express opinions and feelings • Explore new ideas	• Class notes • Discussion notes • Reading notes • Handouts with new info

Materials: Spiral notebook
Colored pens or pencils
Highlighters
Gluestick
Folder (for handouts and assignments not done in the notebook)

Grading: Notebooks will be collected and graded about every four weeks, except at the beginning of the year, when they will be collected after two weeks. Notebooks will be graded on thoroughness, quality, organization, and visual appeal. Students will know the value of each major notebook assignment when it is given. About 30 percent of your grade for the course will be based on your notebook.

Here are the simple guidelines a high school world history teacher has his students follow. Each students receive a copy of these guidelines and is encouraged to glue it to the inside front cover of the notebook.

INTERACTIVE NOTEBOOK GUIDELINES

What is the purpose of the notebook?
The purpose of the interactive notebook is to enable you to be a creative, independent thinker and writer. Interactive notebooks will be used for class notes as well as for other activities where you will be asked to express your own ideas and process the information presented by this class.

What materials do I need?
*Spiral Notebook:
   spiral bound
   college ruled
   70 sheets
   11 X 8 1/2 in.
   white paper
   three-hole punched

*highlighters
*blue or black pens
*gluestick (at home)

How should my notebook be organized?
Your notebook will be organized into a Left Side and a Right Side.

What goes on the Right Side of my notebook?
The Right Side of your notebook is for **class and reading notes**. As you take notes, structure them so that key ideas are clear and supported by examples from either class instruction, discussions, or reading assignments. The Right Side will also be used for **"Here I Stand"** activities in which you will be asked to state conclusions and well-supported personal opinions about the material we have studied in class. "Here I Stand" writings should demonstrate your mastery of the subjects we are studying.

What goes on the Left Side of my notebook?
The Left Side of your notebook will be used for a variety of different activities, **including homework**. This side should be the place where all of your creative and artistic inklings come bursting forth! Left Side activities will ask you to demonstrate your understanding of new ideas. The kinds of activities for the Left Side are listed as follows.
  "RAP": a writing activity where you will be asked to preview new material or review what you have already learned. "RAP" writings are assigned by the instructor.
  "Personal Response": a writing activity where you explore your opinions of and ask questions about class discussions, readings, and activities. "Personal Res[...] instructor or written wh[...] question.

"Working It Out": an activity in which you will be asked to present new ideas in a way that is meaningful to you. For example, you might show your understanding of new ideas by writing a poem or a story, drawing pictures, making diagrams, adding political cartoons, or creating song lyrics. "Working It Out" writings are assigned by the instructor but you will have the choice as to how to express what you have learned.

How will it be possible to earn an "A" on my notebook?
A student who expects to earn an A- or higher grade on the notebook will be one who has taken the time to consistently include extra work. **"Time Out" activities** are unassigned notebook entries which are completed in addition to regular class notebook assignments.

What is a "Time Out" activity?
A "Time Out " activity is one in which you paste related magazine or newspaper articles, pictures, or cartoons into your notebook along with a three or four sentence summary of the material being added. A "Time Out" activity might also be original drawings. Whatever you paste or draw into your notebook should relate to the discussions, readings, and activities we have completed for the class. "Time Out" activities can be included on either the Left or Right Side of the notebook, wherever there is extra space. Sometimes individual pages will also be set aside for "Time Outs". Use "Time Outs" to sharpen the visual appearance of your notebook not to clutter it!

How will my notebook be graded?
Notebooks will be checked periodically for completeness, about every 4 to 6 weeks. All class notes and notebook assignments should be included, even for the days when you were absent. An important part of your notebook is its visual appearance. Your notebook should be neat! Each entry should be titled and dated. Your artistic touch should be visible throughout the notebook.

What happens if I am absent?
If you are absent, it is your responsibility to obtain notebook assignments from either a homework partner or the instructor.

Share this handout with your parent or guardian, then ask them to also sign on the line below.

_____
Student signature

_____
Parent/Guardian signature

Middle school students need particularly well-defined expectations. Here is an example of how one teacher left no room for ambiguity. Notice that the teacher even requested that both the student and a parent or guardian read and sign the guidelines.

Lost Notebooks?

Because students take a lot of pride of ownership in their notebooks, typically very few are lost during a semester. Most teachers report that only a handful of students lose them each year. If your students do lose their notebooks, allow them to make up a select number of assignments so they can receive partial credit.

Organizing Pages

There are many ways to help your students organize their notebooks. Asking them to create an organizing page at the front of their notebooks is an excellent method for helping them keep track of assignments. For example, a table of contents that clearly indicates where assignments are will help you find assignments quickly while evaluating notebooks. There are many ways to arrange an organizing page, from quite simple to more elaborate. Choose the method that best suits you and your students.

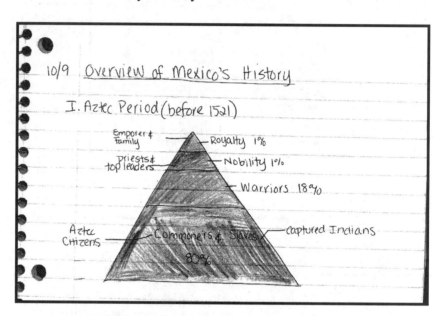

The most important first step to helping students organize their notebooks is making sure they date and create a header for each assignment.

A table of contents can be as simple as a list of completed assignments and page numbers, or it can include more complex information.

Comparative Cultures and Geography

	Date Assigned	Date Due	ASSIGNMENT	Points
1.	5/9	5/18	PATTERNS OF LIFE	10
2.	5/10	5/13	C.E	10
3.	5/11	5/12	HW. HUMMDIINUR QUESTIONS	10
4.	5/16	5/20	CE	10
5.	5/19	1/3	NOTEBOOKS	100
6.	5/23	5/24	NIGERIA READING QUESTIONS	10
7.	5/23	5/27	CE	10
8.	5/31	1/3	CE (Extra Credit)	10
9.	6/2	6/3	Africa & Modern Art	10
10.	6/7		SPEECH	
11.	6/8		Review I	
12.	6/9		Review II	
13.				

This contents page helps students keep track of assignments by number, date, and points earned. It includes both notebook and non-notebook assignments.

UNIT	DATE	HEADING	TITLE	PAGE
			Examples of "working it out" Ideas	1
	8/29	Map	Physiographic Map of the United States	2.
	8/29	Map	States & Capitols	3.
	8/31	Rap	Employer	4
	8/31	Map	World Map	6
	8/31	WOW	Basic Geography	7,8
	9/7	Time-Out	Teacher of American Government fights 'moment of silence' because it may lead to students praying in school	9
	9/7	Time-Out	Calvin and Hobbes	11.
	9/13	Map	Physiographic Map of the United States	14
	9/13	Map	Physiographic	15,17,19
	9/15			

This contents page includes the page numbers where assignments can be found—a great time-saver when it comes time to evaluate notebooks.

GRADE SHEET

ASSIGNMENT	MS. Ross	MY SCORE	MY TOTAL	GRADE	%
Meet Pass	50	50	50	50/50	100%
Scavy Hunt	15	65	14	64	
Quiz	10	75	8	72	
Newsweek	15	90	15	87	87/90	97%
Graph	5	95	5	92	
Xmas 5x5	0	95	4	96	
Dep.-Test	40	135	46	142	
Pop. Profile	20	155	14	156	/155	101%

This organizing page doubles as a grade sheet. It not only keeps track of assignments, but also helps students assess their standing in class.

Help for Absent Students

Keep a master notebook of assignment directions and due dates available at all times to help absent students make up class assignments. Alternatively, ask a student to keep the master notebook, or simply allow students to check the notebooks of their classmates for missed assignments. Make it the students' responsibility to make up incomplete assignments.

Unit Title Pages

For each new unit in the Interactive Student Notebook, have students write the title of the unit on a right-hand page. You might ask them to find a picture or to draw an illustration that represents a theme of the unit. This is an opportunity for students to use their creative genius and to personalize their notebooks.

Cut Out Distracting Student Interruptions

Requiring students to bring their notebooks to class every day will help you cut out interruptions from students who spend time asking classmates for paper, digging through folded papers in their textbooks to search for past assignments, and complaining that they didn't know they needed their notebooks.

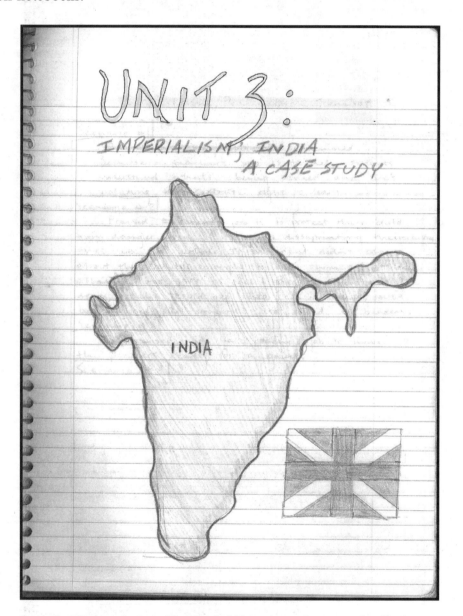

A simple title page design with a few bold images can be extremely effective.

This student created a colorful and complex title page by creating a collage using headlines, letters, graphics, and photographs taken from various publications.

While this student used clever drawings and bright colors for her title page, she found herself caught up in the festive aspects of the 1920s and forgot to include a graphic representation of the Great Depression.

The key to creating effective Interactive Student Notebook assignments is paying careful attention to how you word and present each assignment. Many of the assignments students will be asked to complete—such as creating visual metaphors or reporting on their feelings—are significantly different from traditional assignments. Be prepared to explain and, if necessary, model each assignment. Most importantly, however, pay close attention to how you word the assignment as that is what most students will scrutinize before they begin working in the notebook.

Criteria for Creating Notebook Assignments

These criteria will help you create effective notebook assignments for the right and left sides of your students' notebooks.

- Give **explicit details** about what you expect, including the number of examples, the length of the assignment, and the material to be covered, but be as succinct as possible.

- Use verbs to tell students what to do, such as *draw, outline,* and *create.*

- Explain **where** in the Interactive Student Notebook you expect to see the assignment appear. For example, should it appear on the right or left side of the notebook?

- Tell students specifically **what resources**—the textbook, student notes, outside readings, reference books, interviews, and the like—they can use to complete the assignment.

- Include specific references to the number of **colors** you would like to see in the final assignment.

- Encourage **creativity** and **imagination**.

Create Your Own Terms

Create your own terms for standardized assignments. For example, RAP might stand for a Review and Preview assignment. WIO might stand for a Working It Out assignment, in which students use a summary sentence or spoke diagram to make sense of something they just learned. Some teachers make Current Events a regular assignment. The key is to create terms that will be helpful for your students.

Three Model Assignments

The three model assignments that follow were chosen for their clarity and detail. The teachers who wrote these assignments were inspired by the "Ideas for Student Notebooks" section of this manual, but they added much greater detail for their students.

Mosaic on Latin America's Demography

Pretend you are an artist who has been commissioned (paid) by an important museum to create a mosaic on Latin American demography. (A *mosaic* is a piece of art made with colorful fragments of tile, glass, or quartz that forms a picture or collage.) Use the information from the chart "Generalizations About Latin America Demography" to create a "tile" mosaic that clearly shows the viewer the most important demographic information in Latin America from the chart. Your mosaic should:

- Have an appropriate title.

- Use at least five colors.

- Have "tiles" whose sizes match the importances of the various topics. For example, the tile for Catholicism should be large because the Catholic religion is very important to many people in Latin America.

- Have titles that are (1) rectangles of various sizes adorned with symbols or (2) shaped in the form of symbols that represent the topics (like a church or a cross for Catholicism). Each tile should contain a few key words or phrases and a symbol (if it is not already in the shape of a symbol).

- Use all the information from the chart.

- Show graphical imagination and creativity.

This student used red construction paper to create the tiles of her Latin American mosaic. She created colorful graphics to put on top of the red tiles and paid close to attention to the proportion of the tiles and their basic message.

Address Multiple Intelligences

*Interactive Student Notebooks can tap into **visual intelligence** by including visual elements such as graphs, maps, illustrations, pictowords, and visual metaphors; **musical intelligence** by asking students to compose a song or react to a piece of music in writing; **intrapersonal intelligence** by allowing students to reflect on how history affects them; **interpersonal** strengths by serving as a place to record group discussions or project notes; and **logical-mathematical intelligence** through the use of sequences, graphs, and charts.*

Illustrated Timeline on the Rise of Communist China

On the left side of your notebook, you will create an illustrated timeline of the key events from 1911 to the present in the rise of Communist China. The timeline should go on two or three left-side pages, directly opposite the corresponding lecture notes on the right side. The illustrated timeline will be based on information from

- lecture notes

- the two-page summary of Communist China entitled "The Shifting Winds of Communist China"

- the seven pages of student handouts on the events in the rise of Communist China

- information about Communist China from your textbook—pages 775 to 780

The illustrated timeline should have simple illustrations, graphics, and captions that represent the key ideas in the rise of Communist China. Someone reading the timeline should be able to get a basic understanding of the key events in Communist China.

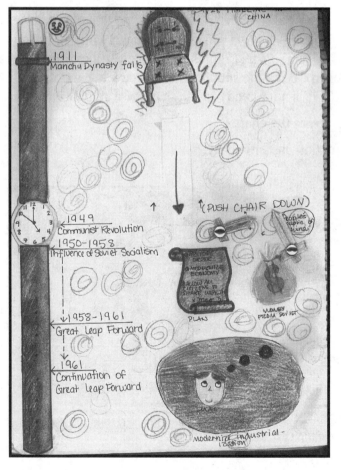

The student who completed this timeline assignment included movable cutouts to emphasize various points. For example, she created two swords battling each other to represent the Communist Revolution and a movable throne to represent the fall of the Manchu Dynasty.

Reading Assignment on the Struggle for Change in Mexico

Read the packet entitled "The Struggle for Change." On two consecutive left pages in your notebook, write the headings "Character Collage of Benito Juarez" and "Character Collage of Porfirio Diaz" and create character collages for these two leaders. Each character collage should include:

- A simple drawing of the figure. It need not look lifelike; a simple body and face will do.

- At least five key words, phrases, or statements that describe the person's background and ideas for how to help Mexico. Place these within or around the figure.

- At least three illustrations or visual symbols that represent the person's background and his ideas for how to help Mexico. Place them within or around the figure.

- At least four colors.

- Lots of creativity and imagination to show what you learned about each leader in the reading.

Someone who looks at your character collages should be able to understand the key ideas and beliefs of Juarez and Diaz. Since Juarez and Diaz had different backgrounds and ideas, your character collages should be quite different. An example of a very good character collage for Martin Luther King Jr. appears on the back of this page.

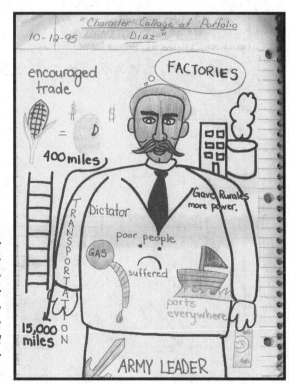

This detailed character collage of Porfirio Diaz is a simple yet powerful way for students to remember and analyze key leadership attributes that can then be compared to those of other Mexican rulers.

Course: Modern World History
Unit: *The Rise and Fall of the Soviet Union*
Activity: "Rock, Scissors, Paper: Understanding Marxist Theory"

Preview 4/13
"Allegory Painting of Class Struggle"

"There's trouble from the lower classes again."

"We must put an end to their begging and whining."

"They're dining in luxury while we work and suffer."

"If we all rise at once, we can break through."

To preview an Experiential Exercise on Marxist theory, students were asked to look at a slide depicting class struggle, make a simple sketch of the slide, and write thought bubbles that show what people from each economic class think of each other.

Student Response 4/13

The teacher told students to look at the same slide depicting class struggle and make a simple sketch of what Marx would say will happen next in the scene. Students wrote thought bubbles that show what people from each economic class think of each other and what the goal of the new society is.

"You took advantage of us for years."

"I earned my wealth. You're just lazy."

"Everyone will be the same economic class now."

Lower Class

Upper Class

Lower Class

Class Notes 4/13
Stages of Marxist Theory

After participating in the Experiential Exercise, which involved students winning and losing while playing rock, paper, scissors, students record notes as the teacher helps them connect their experience to the stages of Marxist theory.

Marxist Theory	Rock, Scissors, Paper Game
CAPITALISM • Private ownership of industry • Freedom of competition • Results in unequal economic classes	**CAPITALISM** • Students started with their own tokens • Students played Rock, Scissors, Paper • Some students won, most lost

↓ ↓

CLASS STRUGGLE
• Upper class and working class struggle over wealth

CLASS STRUGGLE
• Discussed how winners and losers felt

↓ ↓

WORKERS REVOLT
• Working class carries out plan to overtake upper class

WORKERS REVOLT
• Planned to get tokens back (for ex., by stealing) and argued about game's fairness

↓ ↓

SOCIALISM • Government ownership of industry • Goal is to bring economic equality • Aims for a classless society	**SOCIALISM** • Teacher (government) collected tokens • Teacher redistributed tokens equally • Students all have same amount of tokens

↓ ↓

COMMUNISM • Goal of classless society achieved • No government needed	**COMMUNISM** • Students would refuse to play game again and choose to share tokens • Teacher would no longer need to supervise

To preview an Interactive Slide Lecture on Reconstruction following the Civil War, students were asked to write a one-paragraph response to a provocative statement about reconciling friendship.

Preview 5/20

"It's easier to build a new friendship than to reconcile on old friend after a bitter argument." Agree or disagree? Why?

I disagree with this statement. I think both are difficult but that it's generally easier to reconcile with an old friend than to make a new friendship, because you have time spent with each other that you can build on. You may get upset at each other sometimes, but you have past experiences that get you through the hard times.

Processing 5/20
Freedman's Bureau Advertisement

To process historical information, students were asked to create a billboard—using visuals, symbols, and words—that advertises how the Freedman's Bureau planned to assist newly freed African Americans after the Civil War. Students were also asked to add graffiti commenting on the billboard from the perspective of a freed African American.

Freedman's Bureau

Food

Learn reading, writing, and math

What about 40 acres and a mule!!!???

Hospitals

Vote

Teachers from the Abolitionist Movement

Class Notes 5/20
Reconstructing the Nation

Freedman's Bureau

Students recorded notes about the Freedman's Bureau by sketching a slide and annotating it with historical information from the teacher.

Bureau established 4,300 schools.

It educated free men about their rights and responsibilities.

Most bureau agents were from the North and had been involved in the abolitionist movement.

Additional Information about Feedman's Bureau
- 1865—Congress established Freedman's Bureau
- Purpose was to help newly freed African Americans and poor whites in the former Confederacy
- Set up hospitals and rural clinics
- Registered over 700,00 blacks to vote
- Did not distribute "40 acres and a mule" as some leaders advocated
- Distributed over 21 million rations (corn, meal, flour, sugar) to blacks and whites

To preview a Social Studies Skill Builder on World War I propaganda posters, students were asked to describe their favorite advertisement—TV, radio, magazine, or billboard—and what made it memorable.

Describe Your Favorite Advertisement

Describe your favorite advertisement and what makes it memorable.

My favorite TV commercial is the one where the soft drink truck driver tries to sneak a soft drink from the refrigerator and when he grabs one can a bunch of cans come crashing down and everybody is looking at him. It's memorable because it's funny.

Create a Propaganda Poster

Create a poster, label prop tools used, and explain purpose.

Students were asked to select a current events topic—such as AIDS, teen smoking, or presidential elections—and create a propaganda poster to persuade people to do something about the topic. Students were also instructed to label the propaganda tools that were used in the poster and to write a brief statement explaining the purpose of the poster.

Slogan

Would You Want to Kiss This?

Visual Symbol

Quit Smoking
for your boyfriend or girlfriend's sake

Emotional Language

The purpose of my poster is to get young people to think about how gross it is to be around people who smoke.

Comparing Advertising and Wartime Propaganda

	Advertising	Wartime Propaganda
Definition	To call to public attention, especially to sell something	Widespread promotion of particular ideas or beliefs
Purposes	• Buy product • Use services • Support charitable cause • Vote for a candidate	• Enlist in armed services • Buy war bonds • Feel patriotism • Hate/dehumanize enemy • Conserve important resources
Tools	• Humor • Celebrity endorsement • Music • Emotional language • Emotional images	• Humor • Celebrity endorsement • Music • Emotional language • Emotional images

Students recorded notes to compare advertising to wartime propaganda.

Analyzing World War I Propaganda Posters

Placard	Sketch of Poster, Labeled w/ Propaganda Tools Used	Country	Purpose
2.2P	Lend Your Five Shillings To Your Country And / Slogan Emotional Image Crush The Germans Emotional language	England, because "shillings" sounds English	To get people to loan money to their government

Rather than record notes on a separate student handout, students created a matrix and recorded notes on various propaganda posters.

Course: World History
Unit: *Empires and Kingdoms of Sub-Saharan Africa*
Activity: "Understanding Proverbs of the Shona: Lessons for Life"

> *To preview an Experiential Exercise on African proverbs, the teacher told students to analyze a proverb.*

Proverbs

"Don't count your chickens before they're hatched."

What do you think this proverb means?
Don't think you're finished when you're not quite done.

Give an example of a situation where this might be useful advice.
It's like when a basketball team is winning with only a minute left. They shouldn't think they have won. They have to try hard until the end.

What is the purpose of proverbs such as this?
To help you to remember what to do in situations.

Illustrated Proverb for Next Year's Students

"Those who take the greatest risks reap the greatest rewards."

> *Students were asked to create an illustrated proverb for next year's students about how to succeed in this class. Below the proverb, they were instructed to describe a hypothetical situation in which this proverb could be useful to a future student.*

In this class you do things that most students never do in history classes. Sometimes these activities seem weird, but the students who take a risk and get involved end up learning the most. For example, one time our teacher asked for volunteers to come up to a slide on the wall. No one knew what for, but I went up anyway. I ended up becoming the African leader of Timbuktu who was in the slide and telling the class about all the achievements of our empire. Because of that experience, I'll never forget about Timbuktu.

Matrix of Shona Proverbs Activity

Rather than record notes on a separate student handout, students created a matrix and recorded notes as they analyzed various African proverbs.

What's the situation?	What is the proverb?	What does the proverb mean?	How does the proverb relate to the situation?
"Don't do drugs" buttons at school	Setting a mousetrap to catch an elephant is a waste of time.	Big problems are not easily solved.	Jose says buttons are a start but won't solve the problem of drugs at school.
Police warning against skateboarding in an empty pool	The one who refused advice came to be found with a wounded head.	If you pay no attention to advice you will find yourself in trouble.	Shondreka decided to take the advice and not skate.
Tendai is stuck on a math problem	A child who does not cry will die in the sling-cradle.	Speak out if you have a grievance or a want.	Tendai should ask for help when he needs it
Disappointment after receiving a present	To sleep on a worn-out mat is better than sleeping on the bare ground.	Getting something is better than getting nothing at all.	Carly should appreciate the present and try it out.
Boy overhears people making fun of his brother	If an idiot is a member of your own family, you applaud his dancing.	You should be loyal to members of your family.	Vinh should defend his brother.

The following set of notebook assignments encourage active engagement with the History Alive! curriculum. These assignments form the basis of the Interactive Student Notebook. The examples that accompany each type of activity fit in with TCI units and provide a clear picture of how students respond creatively to new information in their notebooks. These assignments can be either teacher generated or student-generated—that is, they can be used on either side of the notebook.

Advertisements

Design advertisements to represent migration, settlement, or the significance of a specific site.

Examples

- Create a classified page that would appeal to nineteenth-century immigrants looking for job opportunities in the United States. Include a title written in bold letters and at least three job listings. For each job listing, include a catchy heading, a two-sentence description of the job, and an appropriate visual.

- Create a page from a travel book that might be used by travelers seeking information about unfamiliar Indian customs. The page should contain a title, brief descriptions of three customs, colorful visuals, and other creative touches.

- Design a real estate advertisement that would encourage people to move to Constantinople in the sixth century.

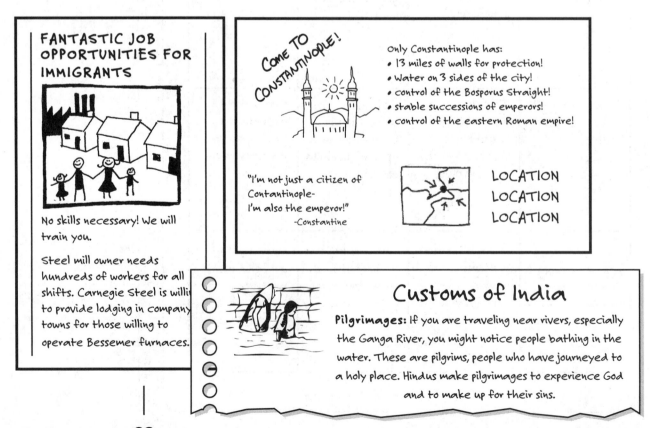

FANTASTIC JOB OPPORTUNITIES FOR IMMIGRANTS

No skills necessary! We will train you.

Steel mill owner needs hundreds of workers for all shifts. Carnegie Steel is willing to provide lodging in company towns for those willing to operate Bessemer furnaces.

Come to Constantinople!

Only Constantinople has:
- 13 miles of walls for protection!
- Water on 3 sides of the city!
- control of the Bosporus Straight!
- stable successions of emperors!
- control of the eastern Roman empire!

"I'm not just a citizen of Contantinople- I'm also the emperor!" -Constantine

LOCATION LOCATION LOCATION

Customs of India

Pilgrimages: If you are traveling near rivers, especially the Ganga River, you might notice people bathing in the water. These are pilgrims, people who have journeyed to a holy place. Hindus make pilgrimages to experience God and to make up for their sins.

Annotated Classroom Maps

Create annotated classroom maps after Experiential Exercises to show how classroom experiences relate to historical situations.

Examples

- Draw an annotated map of the parts of the classroom used in the Experiential Exercise "Experiencing the Struggle to Maintain Unity in the Mauryan Empire." Annotate the map, making connections between the activity and the role the regional kingdoms played in undermining the unity of the Mauryan Empire.

- Draw an annotated classroom map of the parts of the classroom used in the Experiential Exercise "Mapping the Expansion of the Roman Empire." Annotate the map, making connections between the activity and the role the provinces played in strengthening and weakening Rome's empire.

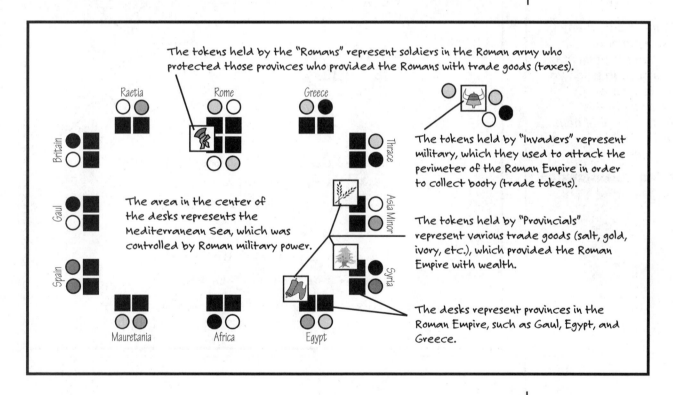

Annotated Illustrations

Make annotated illustrations to recount a story of travel or migration, to represent a moment in time, or to label architectural features.

Examples

- Create a simple illustration of an Inca village. Below your illustration, write a description of a day in the life of a commoner from sunup to sundown.

- Draw a mosque and label its parts.

- Make an annotated illustration of an immigrant's journey from Europe to settlement in the United States.

Model Graphic Thinking

Consider using many of the sample notebook assignments presented in this section when you give class notes. By modeling graphic thinking, you will help your students improve their skills.

Annotated Slides

Use simple sketches of powerful images, accompanied by annotations, to help students understand difficult content.

Examples

- Record notes about the regional ethnic differences in the former Yugoslavia by sketching and annotating a slide of the map of Yugoslavia, Croatia, Slovenia, Macedonia, and Bosnia.

- Record notes about the basic characteristics of Chinese art by sketching and annotating one of the slides from the Response Group activity "Images of Nature: Connecting Painting and Poetry."

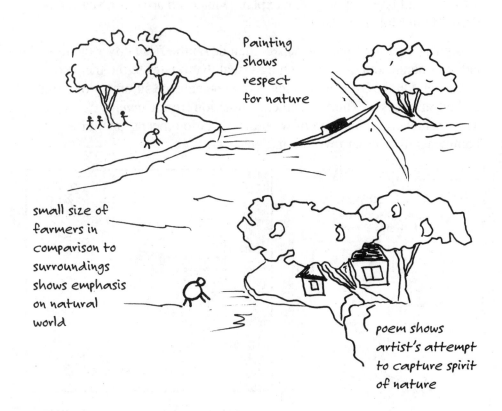

Painting shows respect for nature

small size of farmers in comparison to surroundings shows emphasis on natural world

poem shows artist's attempt to capture spirit of nature

Personal Responses

Personal responses can be used to allow students to express feelings or consider ideas that they might not otherwise share in class. For example, after an activity in which you simulate an assembly in class by having students mass produce drawings of a person, encourage them to write about their personal reactions to the experience. This helps them connect with history and promotes more active learning.

Book or Compact Disk Covers

Design book or compact disk covers to highlight and illustrate important concepts.

Examples

- Create a compact disc cover for the song "La Discriminacion." The cover should include a title and visuals that illustrate important themes and issues in the song.

- Create a cover for an issue of *National Geographic*—using words and graphics—that highlights archeological discoveries made at Mohenjo-Daro. The cover must include an imaginative subtitle, visuals of three artifacts, and brief captions that explain what each artifact reveals about daily life in Mohenjo-Daro.

- Design a cover for *Common Sense*. Include on the front cover the title, the author's name, and an eye-catching visual that relates to the theme of the pamphlet. On the back cover include a two-sentence summary of the life and experiences of Thomas Paine, a quotation from *Common Sense* and a one-sentence explanation of what the quotation means, and three comments from other revolutionary leaders.

Caricatures

Draw caricatures to represent the main characteristics of a group in history or how an individual or group was perceived by another group.

Examples

- Draw a caricature of Alexander Hamilton. Label aspects of the caricature to show his view on these topics: nature of human beings, best type of government, political parties, ideal economy, and view on the Constitution.

- Draw a caricature of Christian armies during the Crusades from a Muslim perspective.

- Draw a caricature of a European immigrant at the turn of the century. Label the immigrant's clothes, possessions, and body parts to show what a typical immigrant might have felt or been prepared for upon arrival to America.

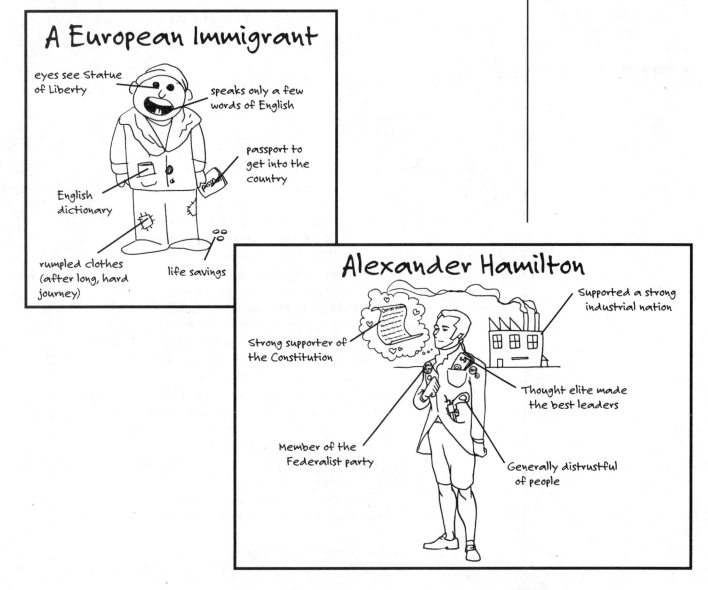

A European Immigrant

- eyes see Statue of Liberty
- speaks only a few words of English
- passport to get into the country
- English dictionary
- rumpled clothes (after long, hard journey)
- life savings

Alexander Hamilton

- Strong supporter of the Constitution
- Supported a strong industrial nation
- Member of the Federalist party
- Thought elite made the best leaders
- Generally distrustful of people

Eulogies

Write eulogies to extol the virtues of prominent historical figures or civilizations.

Examples

- Write a eulogy for the Roman Empire that summarizes the accomplishments of the empire and describes how those accomplishments—in areas such as law, architecture, art, and government—are seen in the world today.

- Write a eulogy for Susan B. Anthony, including an appropriate inscription for her tombstone.

- Write a eulogy for the Ottoman Empire that contains the following words: *millet system, Muslim, sultan, diversity,* and *peace.*

Start Classes Thoughtfully

Put a simple notebook assignment on the board for students to complete as soon as they enter your classroom. The assignment should take only a few minutes to complete. This ritual will ready students to learn and give you time to greet them as they enter.

The Glory of the Ottoman Empire Is Not Forgotten

Oh Sultan, what diversity your majesty governed!
Muslim, Christian, Jew,
So many languages, so many cultures,
All working in harmony because of your brilliant
millet system.
Each faith governed by a leader
overseen by you,
practicing ancient cultures in peace.
Who but the mighty Ottomans could have devised
such a plan of tolerance and cooperation?
The glory of Allah
and the magnificence of the
Mediterranean World
Were showcased in cosmopolitan Constantinople,
Your brilliant capital and crossroads of the world.
But the West could not be sated simply by trade;
The sweet wealth of Ottoman lands
was too tempting.
Arabia's oils, Turkey's ports, the fruits of Palestine
and the wheat of the Nile were too much.
They came, the French and the British
and the Russians,
but they did not understand your
legacy of tolerance.
They sowed division, separation,
and the Ottoman Empire shrunk.

Facial Expressions

Draw facial expressions to summarize the feelings of groups who have different perspectives on a single event.

Examples

- Draw heads and facial expressions of the negotiators from each country represented at the Paris Peace Conference at the end of World War I. Make thought bubbles revealing each leader's goals for the peace treaty.

- Draw heads and facial expressions representing the feelings that hawks, doves, military leaders, and war protesters had about the Vietnam War in 1969. Make thought bubbles above the heads showing what each group might be thinking.

- Draw heads and facial expressions representing the feelings of the Mongols, the Chinese government, and the Chinese peasants after the Mongol invasion. Make thought bubbles above the heads showing what each group might be thinking.

Flow Charts

Create flow charts to show causal relationships or to show steps in a sequence.

Examples

- Create a flow chart that chronicles how the Cold War intensified from 1945 to 1949.

- Create a flow chart that shows the causes of the Russian Revolution.

- Create a flow chart with simple drawings showing how the textile industry grew.

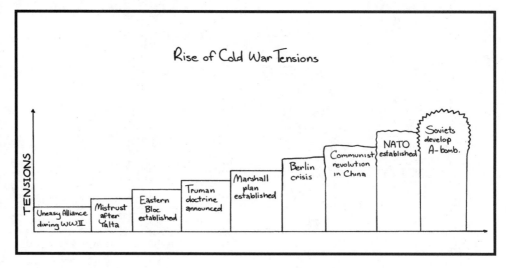

Forms of Poetry

Write various forms of poetry to describe a person, place, event, or feeling of a moment.

Examples

- Write an acrostic using the word *depression* that describes the impact of the Great Depression.

- Write a biographical poem on Buddha that follows this format:
  Line 1: First and last name
  Line 2: Four adjectives describing the Buddha
  Line 3: Relative (son, daughter, husband, wife) of…
  Line 4: Resident of (city and/or country)…
  Line 5: Who lived from (year to year)…
  Line 6: Who searched for…
  Line 7: Who taught…
  Line 8: Who is remembered for…
  Line 9: First and last name

The Buddha
Siddhartha Gautama
Pious, experienced, wise, holy
Son of King Suddhodana and Queen Maya
Resident of India near the Himalayas
Who lived during the fifth century BC
Who searched for enlightenment
Who taught moderation through the Eightfold Path
Who is remembered for developing a belief system
still important today
Final name of Buddha means Enlightened One

D evastating
E conomic collapse
P overty strikes
R eality grim
E verywhere
S avings lost
S adness grows
I nsecurity mounts
O minous
N owhere to turn.

Historical Journals

Assume the role of a historical figure to keep a journal that recounts the figure's feelings and experiences in language of the era.

Examples

- Pretend you are a Confederate soldier at the beginning of the Civil War who has relatives living in the North. Explain why you are fighting for the Confederacy and what you will do if you encounter a relative on the battlefield.

- Pretend you are an Arab traveler on the Silk Road to China. Write a travel log that describes the highlights of your trip.

- Pretend you are a peasant, a noble, or a member of the clergy during the radical stage of the French Revolution. Keep a journal of how the events of this stage affect you.

Historical Markers

Create historical markers to summarize important historical events.

Examples

- Create a historical marker for the Alamo. The marker should include a drawing of the Alamo, a succinct summary of the events that transpired there in 1836, and a brief explanation of the Alamo's significance in the history of the Southwest.

- Create a historical marker to commemorate the birthplace of Siddhartha Gautama, the Buddha. The marker should include a picture of Siddhartha from some stage in his life, a brief summary of his life, and an explanation of the importance of his life in the history of Asia.

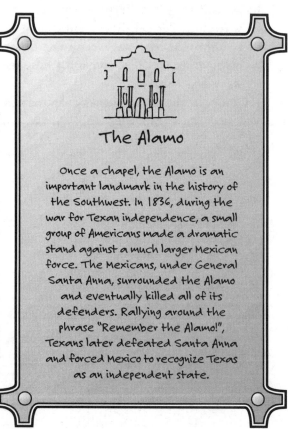

The Alamo

Once a chapel, the Alamo is an important landmark in the history of the Southwest. In 1836, during the war for Texan independence, a small group of Americans made a dramatic stand against a much larger Mexican force. The Mexicans, under General Santa Anna, surrounded the Alamo and eventually killed all of its defenders. Rallying around the phrase "Remember the Alamo!", Texans later defeated Santa Anna and forced Mexico to recognize Texas as an independent state.

Illustrated Dictionary Entries

Explain key terms by creating illustrated dictionary entries. Write a definition, provide a synonym and an antonym, and draw an illustration to represent each term.

Examples

- Create an illustrated dictionary entry for the term *samsara,* which means enlightenment. Define the term in your own words, provide a synonym and an antonym, and draw an illustration that represents the term.

- Create an illustrated dictionary entry for the term *monopoly*. Define the term in your own words, provide a synonym and an antonym, and draw an illustration that represents the term.

Monopoly

definition: to have total control
of something, such as an
industry

synonym: cartel

antonym: competition

Students React to Current Events

Ask students to cut out a newspaper or magazine article (or to summarize a television or radio report) relevant to the history they are learning. Have them paste the article on the left-hand side of their notebooks. Then, challenge them to write a paragraph that connects the current event to the history they are learning.

Illustrated Outlines

Use simple drawings and symbols to graphically highlight and organize class notes.

Examples

- Create a simple symbol for each step of the French Revolution. Draw the symbol in the margin alongside class notes explaining the specific stage of the revolution.

- Use simple sketches for each main topic to help record notes about the relationship between Native Americans and the land.

Development of Native American Cultures

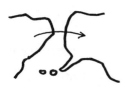   

Migrated from Asia

- encouraged by pursuit of big game hunting
- traveled across the Bering Strait
- migrated approximately 20,000–50,000 years ago

Migrated into Eight Geographic Regions

- California
- Northwest Coast
- Plateau
- Great Basin
- Southwest
- Great Plains
- Eastern Woodlands
- Southeast

Adapted to Environment

- built shelter using materials from surroundings
- managed freshwater resources responsibly
- developed special tools for hunting and food production
- produced clothing compatible with environment

Created Unique Cultures

- Comanche
- Hopi
- Inuit
- Sioux
- Nez Percé

Illustrated Proverbs

Create illustrated proverbs to explain complex concepts.

Example

- Complete this statement, "The Loyalist arguments against colonial independence are best represented by the proverb…" by choosing one of the following proverbs or creating one of your own: *Don't bite the hand that feeds you. Children should respect their elders. Don't cut off your nose to spite your face.* Below the proverb, make a simple drawing of the proverb and label the historical comparisons.

The Loyalist Proverb

Children (the American colonies) should respect their elders (England) because they provide:

clothing and other manufactured goods

shelter and security

food

England

American Colonies

Model Assignments

Innovative notebook assignments like these will be new to most students. To set students up for success, model each new type of assignment. Before asking them to create a sensory figure, for example, model one on an overhead transparency.

Illustrated Timelines

Create illustrated timelines to sequence a series of events in chronological order.

Examples

- Create an illustrated timeline—with a symbol, illustration, or picture for each event—of the eight stages we studied of the Holocaust.

- Create an illustrated timeline—with a symbol, illustration, or picture for each event—of the events leading to the American Revolution.

- Create an illustrated timeline—with a symbol, illustration, or picture for each event—of the major steps in the evolution of democracy.

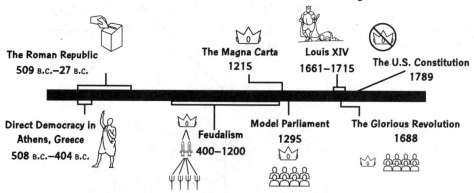

The Evolution of Democracy

Invitations

Design invitations that highlight the main goals and salient facts of important historical events.

Examples

- Design an invitation that might be sent to prospective participants in a conference held to debate how the resources of the Brazilian rainforest should be used. The invitation should include information about when the convention will begin and end, who will be participating, where it will be held, and what will be accomplished. Invitations should include a bold title, an eye-catching visual, and other creative touches common in formal invitations.

- Design an invitation that might be sent to prospective delegates to the Constitutional Convention. The invitation should include information about when the convention will begin and end, where it will take place, who has been invited, and what will be accomplished at the meeting. Invitations must include a bold title, a catchy statement to entice delegates to attend, and other creative touches common in formal invitations.

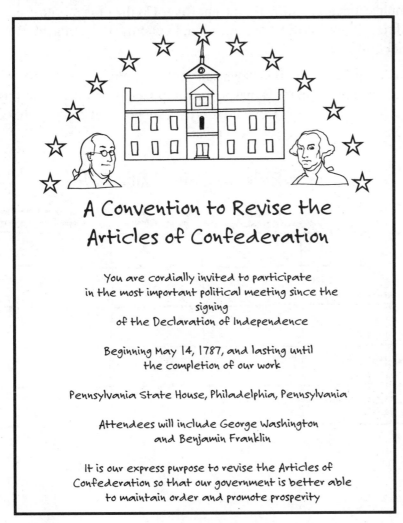

A Convention to Revise the Articles of Confederation

You are cordially invited to participate
in the most important political meeting since the signing
of the Declaration of Independence

Beginning May 14, 1787, and lasting until
the completion of our work

Pennsylvania State House, Philadelphia, Pennsylvania

Attendees will include George Washington
and Benjamin Franklin

It is our express purpose to revise the Articles of
Confederation so that our government is better able
to maintain order and promote prosperity

Making Connections Outside the Classroom

After completing an activity, find examples outside of class of the topic or concept studied.

Examples

• Find an example of a tessellation in your community, such as might be seen in a building, a piece of fabric, or computer art. Make a sketch of the tessellation, write a description of it, and identify the geometric shapes that compose the tessellation.

• Choose a contemporary song and write about the African musical traditions present in the song. List at least three traditions.

Save Paper

Require students to draw simple matrices, charts, and maps in their notebooks. This will cut down on the number of student handouts you need to reproduce.

Matrices

Complete matrices to organize large bodies of information.

Examples

• Complete a matrix entitled "Ancient River Civilizations" with these headings: River Civilization, Location, Economy, Government, Religion, Social Structure.

• Complete a matrix entitled "Dynastic Rule in China, A.D. 589–1644" with these headings: Chinese Dynasty, Territory Controlled, How did this dynasty rise to power?, How did this dynasty govern China?, What belief systems were encouraged/discouraged?

Dynastic Rule in China, A.D. 589–1644

Chinese Dynasty	Territory Controlled	How did this country rise to power?	How did this dynasty govern China?	What belief system were encouraged / discouraged?
Sui (A.D. 589–618)				
Tang (A.D. 618–907)				
Song (A.D. 960–1279)				
Yuan (A.D. 1260–1368)				
Ming (A.D. 1368–1644)				

Metaphorical Representations

Create metaphorical representations to explain difficult or abstract historical concepts.

Examples

- Complete this statement: *The scramble for African territory among European powers was like...* using one of the following analogies or one of your own: prospectors racing to stake a claim in the gold country, concertgoers clamoring for the best seats, or sharks in a feeding frenzy. Make a simple drawing of your analogy and label the historical comparisons.

- Complete this statement: *The three branches of government under the Constitution are like...* using one of the following analogies or one of your own: a three-ring circus, a football team, a musical band, or a three-part machine. Make a simple drawing of your analogy and label the historical comparisons.

- Complete this statement: *Enacting the New Deal was like...* using one of the following analogies or one of your own: putting a small bandage on a gushing wound, creating a safety net to stop falling objects, or demolishing a building that only needed to be repainted. Make a simple drawing of your analogy and label the historical comparisons.

- Complete this statement: *The many changes in communist policies in China were like...* using one of the following analogies or one of your own: shifting winds, a seesaw, a tennis game. Make a simple drawing of the analogy and label the historical comparisons.

Mind Notes

Draw and label outlines of the heads of important historical figures. Fill in the outline with quotations and paraphrased thoughts from the figure.

Examples

- Draw and label a simple outline of the heads of Lenin and Stalin. After discussing the main ideas of these two figures, write important quotations and paraphrased beliefs in the appropriate outline.

- Draw and label a simple outline of the heads of Thomas Jefferson and George Washington. After discussing critical-thinking questions relating to the ideas of these two, write important quotations and paraphrased beliefs in the appropriate outline.

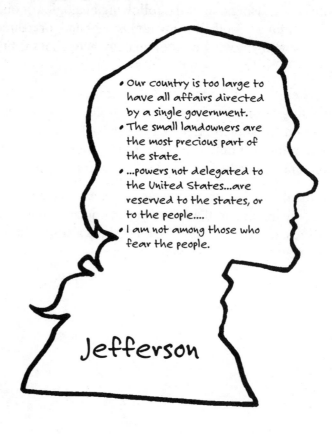

- Our country is too large to have all affairs directed by a single government.
- The small landowners are the most precious part of the state.
- ...powers not delegated to the United States...are reserved to the states, or to the people....
- I am not among those who fear the people.

Jefferson

Mosaics

Synthesize information from a broad content area by creating mosaics. Use visuals and words to represent similarities, differences, and important concepts.

Examples

- Create a mosaic on Latin America demography. The mosaic should include an appropriate title, at least five colors, "tiles" whose sizes and shapes match the importance of the various topics, key words or phrases and a symbol on each tile, and graphics that show imagination and creativity.

- Create a mosaic to summarize key details on how Native Americans adapted to their environment. The mosaic should include an appropriate title, at least five colors, "tiles" containing visuals of different environmental adaptations, key words or phrases that describe each visual, and graphics that show imagination and creativity.

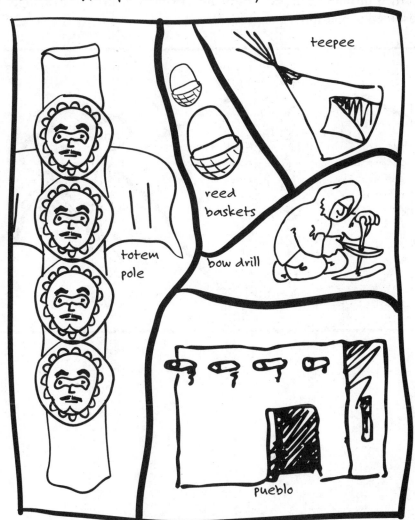

Mosaic of Adaptations Made by Native Americans

Perspective Pieces

Design drawings or write newspaper articles to represent different perspectives on controversial figures, events, and concepts.

Examples

- Create a Janus figure—a drawing based on the Roman god portrayed with two opposite faces—to represent the English and French perspectives of Joan of Arc. Label each part of the figure and explain its symbolism.

- Design a commemorative plaque for Hernan Cortes from the Spanish perspective. Then, design a "Wanted" poster for him from the Aztec perspective.

- Write two newspaper articles summarizing the bombardment of Ft. Sumter. The first article should represent the perspective of a Union journalist, and the second should represent the opposing Confederate viewpoint.

- Draw a simple representation of a pioneer and a Native American and list their different perspectives on the advantages and disadvantages of westward expansion.

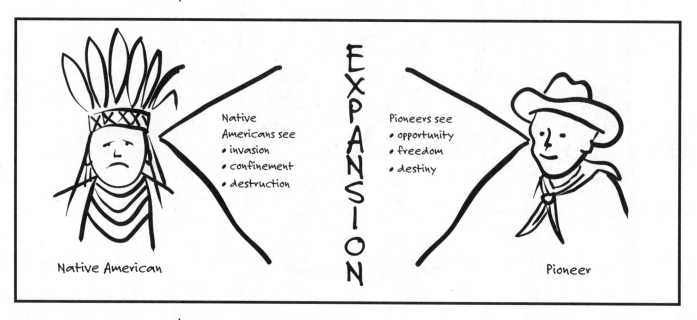

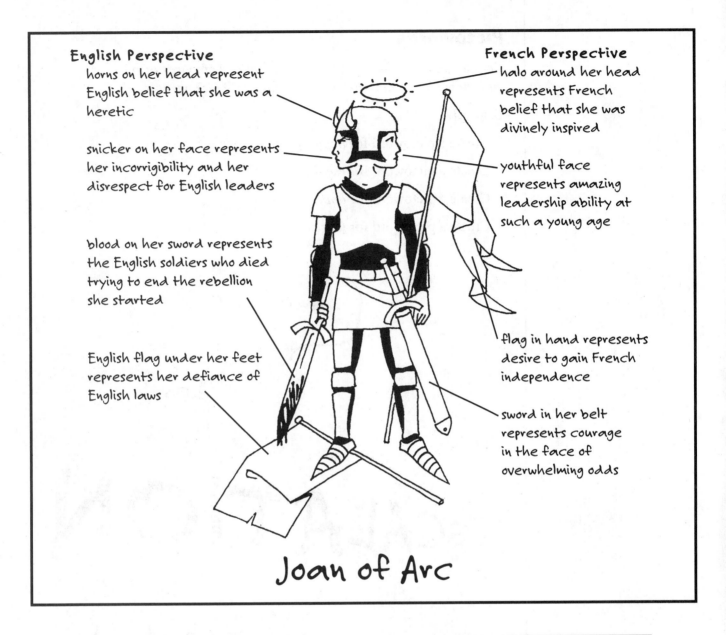

English Perspective

horns on her head represent English belief that she was a heretic

snicker on her face represents her incorrigibility and her disrespect for English leaders

blood on her sword represents the English soldiers who died trying to end the rebellion she started

English flag under her feet represents her defiance of English laws

French Perspective

halo around her head represents French belief that she was divinely inspired

youthful face represents amazing leadership ability at such a young age

flag in hand represents desire to gain French independence

sword in her belt represents courage in the face of overwhelming odds

Joan of Arc

A NATIONAL HERO:

Hernan Cortés

All of Spain should recognize the great accomplishments of Hernan Cortés, a hero to us all.

- conquered Aztecs
- expanded Spain's claim to the new world.
- helped spread Christianity
- aquired gold and riches

WANTED:

Hernan Cortés

Be on the lookout for this ruthless, evil murderer, thief, and threat to the Aztec people. Cortés is wanted for:

- Murder of thousands of Aztecs
- Destruction of Tenochtitlan
- Enslaving innocent people.
- Robbery of gold and relics

Pictowords

Create pictowords—symbolic representations of words or phrases that show their meaning—to help define difficult concepts.

Examples

- Create a pictoword for *imperialism.*

- Create a pictoword for *escalation.*

- Create a pictoword for *appeasement.*

- Create a pictoword for *fascism.*

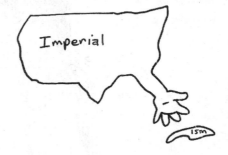

ESCALATION

appeasement

fascißm

Political Cartoons and Comic Strips

Create political cartoons and comic strips to provide social or political commentary on important historical events.

Examples

- Create a political cartoon that comments on the relationship between the North and the South on the eve of the Civil War. As symbols for the North and South, you may use siblings, a wife and husband, neighbors, or images of your own.

- Create a comic strip that depicts the steps involved in the silent trading of gold and salt in tenth-century West Africa. Captions or voice bubbles for the comic strip should contain these terms: *North African, Wangaran, Soninke, gold, salt, Sahara Desert, Niger River,* and *Ghana.*

Postcards

After studying specific content, write postcards to summarize information about places or events.

Examples

- Assume the role of a colonist who has settled in one of the 13 colonies in the early eighteenth century. Write a postcard to a friend in Europe describing the colony in which you have settled. Describe the key features of the colony and the colonists' reasons for settling there. Create an image for the reverse side of the postcard that includes visuals, maps, or other graphics that highlight interesting aspects of the colony.

- Write a postcard to Stalin from Magnitogorsk as if you were John Scott in 1937. On the reverse side, draw a visual that might have appeared on a postcard of Magnitogorsk at that time.

Posters

Draw posters to emphasize key points about political ideas, a political figure's point of view, or reasons behind important historical events.

Examples

- Create a campaign poster that might have been used in the election of 1828. The poster should list Andrew Jackson's qualifications for the presidency, include a memorable campaign slogan, and employ colorful visuals. At the bottom of the poster include graffiti that opponents of Jackson might have scrawled on such a poster.

- Create a recruiting poster to encourage Europeans to participate in the first crusade to the Holy Land. Include at least three reasons for going, each accompanied by a visual.

Provocative Statements

Have students react to provocative statements to introduce historical themes or to critically assess a historical period.

Examples

- "Only the wealthy and the educated should be able to govern." Write a paragraph that supports or refutes that statement.

- "Manifest Destiny was justified." Write an essay that supports or refutes that statement.

- "Communism improved life in Russia." Write an essay that supports or refutes that statement.

Report Cards

Use graded evaluations to assess the policies of leaders or governments.

Examples

- Evaluate the Allies' response during World War II. Give a letter grade—A+, A, A–, B+, and so on—and a corresponding written explanation on each of these topics: policy toward Germany before 1939, effectiveness of military actions, response to the Holocaust, and concern for enemy civilians given wartime conditions.

- Evaluate Hatshepsut's performance as a pharaoh. Give a letter grade—A+, A, A–, B+, and so on—and a corresponding written explanation on each of these topics: expanding the empire, fostering trade with other peoples, and balancing the power among different groups in Egypt.

Sensory Figures

Create sensory figures—simple drawings of prominent historical figures with descriptions of what they might be seeing, hearing, saying, feeling, or doing—to show the thoughts, feelings, and experiences of historical figures.

Examples

- Create a sensory figure for Mansa Musa's pilgrimage to Makkah.

- Create a sensory figure for Lady Murasaki Shikibu that represents daily life in Japan's Imperial Court during the eleventh century.

- Create sensory figures for Malcolm X and Martin Luther King Jr. that show how their different backgrounds and experiences shaped their respective philosophies.

- Create a sensory figure for Elizabeth Cady Stanton after the Seneca Falls Convention.

I have spoken with Es-Saheli a Muslim architect, and asked him to return with me to Mali to help redesign our cities.

As I listen to the prayers in the Mosque I am reminded that the language of Arabic helps unite all Muslims.

I believe with all my heart that there is no God but Allah, and Muhammad is his prophet.

To fulfill the Muslim obligation of zakat, I distributed gold to the people of Cairo with my own hands.

My feet have walked over 3,500 miles to reach the holy city of Makkah.

I have heard rumors that some of the people living in the countryside are envious of our comfortable lifestyle here at Heian.

I am careful never to laugh with my mouth open because it is considered quite rude.

I saw two courtiers using black and white tiles to play Go, a chinese board game.

Since we nobles often make our own perfume, it is possible for me to identify my friends by their fragrence alone.

It warmed my heart to learn that one of my closest friends is engaged to a member of the royal family.

I love the feel of my beautiful silk robes.

My feet long to venture beyond the halls of the court at Heian someday.

Spectrums

Place information on spectrums to show multiple perspectives on a topic or to express an opinion about an issue.

Examples

- Draw a spectrum ranging from "Favors Capitalism" to "Favors Socialism." Place the major political and industrial figures from 1890 to 1940 that we have studied—Eugene Debs, Henry Ford, Emma Goldman, Herbert Hoover, John L. Lewis, Huey Long, John D. Rockefeller, Franklin Roosevelt, Teddy Roosevelt, and Booker T. Washington—at the appropriate places on the spectrum.

- Draw a spectrum ranging from "Praiseworthy Motive" to "Condemnable Motive." Place each of the five motives for European imperialism—economic, political, religious, ideological, and exploratory—on the appropriate part of the spectrum. Write a one-sentence justification for your placement of each motive.

- Draw a spectrum ranging from "Abolish Slavery Now" to "Keep Slavery Forever." Use information from your textbook to determine where to place John C. Calhoun, Abraham Lincoln, and Harriet Tubman.

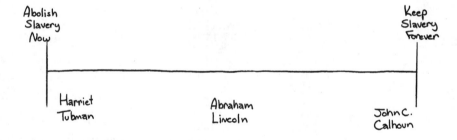

Get Great Color

Here are some ways to encourage students to use color:

- *Require them to purchase highlighters and colored pencils.*
- *Include the use of color as a criterion for completing assignments.*
- *Showcase notebooks with good use of color.*
- *Encourage students to review readings or class notes using highlighters to emphasize key points.*

Spoke Diagrams

Create spoke diagrams as a visual alternative to outlining.

Examples

- Make spoke diagrams showing the major features of Kilwa, the Kongo Kingdom, and the Zimbabwe state.

- Make an illustrated spoke diagram depicting aspects of life of three prominent ethnic groups in Nigeria at the end of the nineteenth century: the Hausa-Fulani, the Igbo, and the Yoruba.

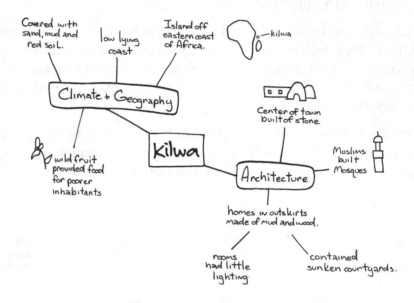

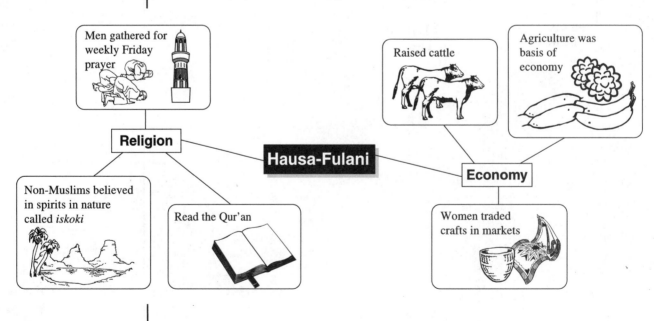

T-Charts

Create T-charts to compare classroom experiences with historical details, to look at advantages and disadvantages of a topic, or to compare and contrast two different items.

Examples

- Create a T-chart that connects specific experiences from the Experiential Exercise activity "Experiencing the Struggle to Maintain Unity in the Mauryan Empire" with historical details from the period.

- Create a T-chart that compares and contrasts the life histories and beliefs of Martin Luther King Jr. and Malcolm X.

In-class Experience	History of India 184 B.C.E. to 320 C.E.
• Blue, Green, Orange, and Red groups earned tokens by crossing chairs blindfolded • Purple group earned tokens by assisting other groups across chairs • Purple group assisted all groups across chairs in round 1 of the activity • Purple group earned lots of tokens in round 1 of the activity • Some groups earned more tokens by crossing chairs without assistance • Some groups chose to cross the chairs without assistance from the Purple group	• Regional kingdoms produced goods that could be traded for profit • Mauryan leaders collected taxes from regional kingdoms in exchange for protection • Early Mauryan leadership effectively governed regional kingdoms • Mauryan leaders profited from their control of regional kingdoms • Kingdoms that traded independently with foreign nations became wealthy • Regional kingdoms eventually broke away from the Mauryan Empire

Venn Diagrams

Create Venn diagrams to compare and contrast people, concepts, places, or groups.

Examples

- Make a Venn diagram comparing and contrasting imperial China and feudal Japan.

- Make a Venn diagram comparing and contrasting the North and the South before the Civil War.

- Make a Venn diagram comparing the perspectives of Union, Confederate, and African-American soldiers on the Civil War.

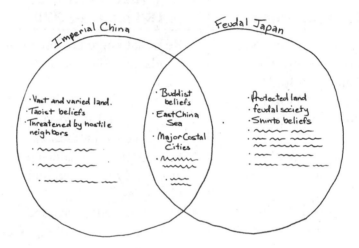

Imperial China

- Vast and varied land.
- Taoist beliefs
- Threatened by hostile neighbors

Feudal Japan

- Protected land
- feudal society
- Shinto beliefs

- Buddist beliefs
- East China Sea
- Major Costal Cities

Union Soldiers
- initially excited about joining; thought conflict would be brief and decisive

All Three
- endured suffering created by inferior medical practices
- initially excited about joining but became less motivated over time
- viewed war as ugly and grim instead of romantic and exciting

Confederate Soldiers
- believed they were fighting for independence; only wanted to defend homes

African-American Soldiers
- saw better opportunities as cooks, drivers, scouts, and soldiers for Union

"What If?" Statements

Use "What if?" statements to apply newfound knowledge to hypothetical historical situations.

Examples

- What if women had the same rights as men in the United States over time? Explain the ways in which the course of American history might have been different.

- What if the Industrial Revolution had occurred first in Africa, not in Europe? Describe how you think the course of history in Africa and Europe might have changed.

- What if India did not have a caste system? Describe how you think peasant farmers might have reacted to their plight if they were not part of a caste system.

- What if Malcolm X and Martin Luther King Jr. had not been assassinated? Describe how you think the course of history in the United States might have changed.

- What if you had been drafted to fight in the Vietnam War? Explain how you would have felt and what you would have done.

An effective system for assessing notebooks will keep the task from becoming burdensome and time consuming. This section contains suggestions to help you manage the load of assessing student notebooks so that students can receive regular, helpful feedback.

Daily Evaluation Suggestions

Here are some ways you can assess notebooks on a daily basis, thus saving yourself time during more formal evaluation of notebooks.

- Glance at notebooks during class each day for the first two weeks of the semester. Walk around the classroom while students are working and give positive comments and helpful suggestions. This is important early in the year and from time to time throughout the year. Otherwise, students may get careless, and the quality of their notebooks will suffer.

- Ask students to work on another assignment as you walk around the classroom and check their homework from the night before. Give each student a mark (0 = not done; ✓ = needs work; ÷ = average effort; and + = excellent) or a special stamp. This will help ensure they do their homework on time and not just before their notebooks are due.

- Pass out a model of outstanding notes for a particular lecture or activity. Put students into groups of two and have them evaluate their notebooks according to the model.

- On occasion, allow students to use their notebooks to take a quiz. If their notes are good, their grades should reflect this.

Use a Homework Stamp

Get a unique stamp and use it to stamp completed homework assignments the day they are due. This is a quick way to assess student work and to make sure assignments are completed on time.

Formal Evaluations

Some teachers formally evaluate notebooks every three to four weeks. Others collect the notebooks after each quarter. However often you decide to formally assess notebooks, here are some suggestions for making the process easy on you and meaningful for students.

- If you use Interactive Student Notebooks in all your classes, don't collect them all at once—stagger their collection so that you only have to grade one class set at a time.

- Don't feel compelled to grade every notebook entry. Carefully evaluate the most important entries and spot-check other assignments.

- At the beginning of the semester, clearly explain to students the criteria on which their notebooks will be evaluated. This may include the quality and completeness of assignments, visual appearance and organization, and extra credit assignments.

- To aid in assessing the notebooks, create a notebook evaluation sheet and distribute it to students to fill out before they turn in their notebooks. Two model evaluation sheets follow. Use them as a basis for creating your own evaluation sheet.

- Require students to do a self-assessment of their notebooks. This enables them to reflect on their learning and to critically review their progress. Explain that if your assessment is markedly different from theirs—either better or worse—they will have the opportunity to discuss with you the reasons for your assessment. Make it clear that ultimately your grade is binding. In the vast majority of cases, students assess their notebooks fairly—or are harder on themselves than you are.

Get Students off to the Right Start

Don't wait until late in the semester to check student notebooks. Either check individual assignments immediately by walking around the room and quickly reading them, or collect notebooks within the first few weeks of class to make sure students get off to the right start.

Notebook Evaluation Models

The notebook evaluation sheet below is one example of a handout that will help you assess your students' work. In the "Notebook Assignment" column, list the assignments you want to grade. (To lighten your grading load, list only a portion of the total number of assignments you expected students to complete.) Distribute the evaluation sheet to students, and have them assess their notebooks before they turn them in to you. This enables them to reflect on their learning and to critically review their notebook entries and organization.

Reduce Paper Flow

Tired of stacks of ungraded student papers covering your desk? Having students use Interactive Student Notebooks can dramatically reduce your paper load. Students complete several weeks of assignments in their notebooks before you collect them. Once you collect them, selectively assess assignments. This significantly reduces the time you spend collecting, assessing, recording, and returning student assignments.

Name _____

Notebook Evaluation Sheet

Directions: Before turning in your notebook, grade yourself on each of the assignments below as well as on Visual Appearance and Extra Credit. Grade yourself fairly and honestly; I will grade you as well. I will clearly tell you what I am looking for. Keep in mind that my grade is binding, but if there is a discrepancy, you may politely arrange a time to meet with me to discuss the difference in assessment. After we meet, I reserve the right to change the grade if I made an error in judgment; however, I also reserve the right to stick by my original grade.

Notebook Assignment	Due Date	Possible Points	Student Assessment	Teacher Assessment
Character Collages on Chinese Beliefs	9/8	15	13	14
Class Notes on Chinese Beliefs	9/9	10	10	9
Compare Dynastic/Communist China	9/10	8	6	7
Class Notes on Rise of Communism	9/10	5	5	5
Illustrated Timeline of Communist China	9/12	15	13	12
Feelings on China Debate	9/13	10	9	9
Notes on Textbook Reading pp. 123–8	9/14	8	7	6
Extra Credit		20	15	18
Visual Appearance		15	13	12
Totals		106	91	92

Student Comments: I don't know how well I did. This notebook was kind of a pain at times. I think I included everything you asked for, but they were some weird assignments. I think this notebook will help me remember things for a long time.

Teacher Comments: You did a good, solid job on this notebook. Keep in mind that you can use more of your excellent visuals for extra credit. You really used the left side of the notebook well to make sense of what you were learning in class.

After students have graded their own notebooks, collect them and grade them yourself. You need not grade every notebook entry for the unit or grading period. Instead, carefully evaluate some of the most important entries and spot-check a few of the other assignments for quality and thoroughness. In addition, assess aesthetic appearance and student-initiated extra credit assignments. Criteria for aesthetic appearance include neatness, organization, effective use of color, and appropriate use of highlighters. Student-initiated extras include newspaper clippings, illustrations, and personal responses to news items.

Some teachers prefer a more holistic approach to evaluating notebooks that requires even less time. The evaluation sheet below gives a single score for three major criteria.

Beyond the Minimum

Encourage your students to go beyond the minimum requirements for notebooks by setting high standards. Give a B for a complete notebook and an A for exceptional work beyond the basic requirements.

Name _____

Notebook Evaluation Sheet

	Student Evaluation	Teacher Evaluation

Quality and Completeness
- All class notes and right-side work are completed and of high quality, even for days when you are absent
- All left-side work is completed and of high quality

20	25	30	35	40	44
Needs Improvement			Fair	Good	Excellent

Student Evaluation: **40**   Teacher Evaluation: **41**

Visual Appearance and Organization
- Left- and right-side work is organized and neat
- Effective highlighting and use of color

20	25	30	35	40	44
Needs Improvement			Fair	Good	Excellent

Student Evaluation: **42**   Teacher Evaluation: **35**

Extra Credit
- Newspaper cutouts, drawings, graphics, or unassigned personal responses
- Other items

0	2	4	6	8	10	12
Needs Improvement			Fair	Good	Excellent

Student Evaluation: **6**   Teacher Evaluation: **8**

Student Comments
I liked doing this notebook. It really helped me think about China. But I don't know how good my drawings were.

Total   Student: **88**   Teacher: **84**

Teacher Comments
Great job. Next time, think about your visuals a little more. You don't need to be a great artist, but try to make your visuals include more historical details.